OXFORD
UNIVERSITY PRESS

A New World at the Library

M. J. Cosson

Illustrated by Adrian Mateescu

OXFORD
UNIVERSITY PRESS

198 Madison Avenue
New York, NY 10016 USA

Great Clarendon Street, Oxford OX2 6DP UK

Oxford University Press is a department of the University of Oxford. It furthers the University's objective of excellence in research, scholarship, and education by publishing worldwide in

Oxford   New York
Auckland Cape Town Dar es Salaam
Hong Kong Karachi Kuala Lumpur Madrid
Melbourne Mexico City Nairobi New Delhi
Shanghai Taipei Toronto

With offices in
Argentina Austria Brazil Chile Czech Republic
France Greece Guatemala Hungary Italy Japan
Poland Portugal Singapore South Korea
Switzerland Thailand Turkey Ukraine Vietnam

OXFORD and OXFORD ENGLISH are registered trademarks of Oxford University Press.

Photocopying

The Publisher grants permission for the photocopying of those pages marked "photocopiable" according to the following conditions. Individual purchasers may make copies for their own use or for use by classes that they teach. School purchasers may make copies for use by staff and students, but this permission does not extend to additional schools or branches.

Under no circumstances may any part of this book be photocopied for resale.

Any websites referred to in this publication are in the public domain and their addresses are provided by Oxford University Press for information only. Oxford University Press disclaims any responsibility for the content.

Executive Publishing Manager: Stephanie Karras
Managing Editor: Sharon Sargent
Design Manager: Stacy Merlin
Project Coordinator: Sarah Dentry
Production Layout Artist: Colleen Ho
Cover Design: Colleen Ho, Stacy Merlin, Michael Steinhofer
Manufacturing Manager: Shanta Persaud
Manufacturing Controller: Eve Wong

ISBN: 978 0 19474030 2 (BOOK)

ISBN: 978 0 19474039 5 (OPD READING LIBRARY)

ISBN: 978 0 19474058 6 (ACADEMICS READING LIBRARY)

Printed in China

10 9 8 7 6 5 4

Many thanks to Pronk&Associates, Kelly Stern, and Meg Brooks for a job well done.

This book is printed on paper from certified and well-managed sources.

A New World at the Library

Table of Contents

A. Match the pictures with the words.

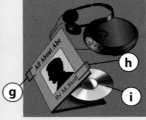

__i__ 1. audiobook	____ 5. magazine	____ 9. self-checkout
____ 2. author	____ 6. newspaper	____ 10. title
____ 3. DVD	____ 7. online catalog	
____ 4. library clerk	____ 8. picture book	

B. Answer the questions.

1. What can you check out at a library?
2. What other things can you do at a library?
3. Do you have a library card?
4. What kinds of books do you read?
5. What is your favorite magazine?

C. Read the title of this book. Look at the pictures in the book. Then guess the answers to the questions. Circle *a* or *b*.

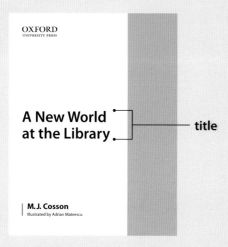

1. Where does this story happen?
   a. This story happens in a bookstore.
   b. This story happens in a library.

2. Who is this book about?
   a. This book is about Eva.
   b. This book is about Diego.

Chapter 1

Books Everywhere!

I'm inside the library, and I see books everywhere. Most of the books are in English. I'm nervous!

A library clerk asks, "Can I help you?"

"Yes," I answer. "I need a library card."

I show my student ID card. The card has my name and my address. It also has a picture of me. I fill out a form. Then I sign my name. The library clerk gives me a library card.

The library clerk smiles and says, "Eva, we have books and many other things here. Please ask questions if you need help."

"Thank you," I answer.

"You're welcome," the library clerk says. "You can check out four books today. You can keep them for two weeks. You can also check out an audiobook or a DVD. Next time, you can check out 30 books."

"That's a lot of books!" I say.

Library Application Form

Name: Eva Velazquez

Address: 5616 Alamo Dr.

Austin, TX 78738

Telephone Number: (512) 555-1234

Email: e_velazquez@mail.us

Signature: Eva Velazquez

I see a man using the self-checkout. He checks out six books.

"Do I need to check out 30 books next time?" I ask the library clerk.

"Oh, no," she says. "That's the number you *can* check out. You don't have to check out 30. You can bring the books back early, too. There's a fine for late books."

LATE FINES

BOOKS $0.15 A DAY

AUDIOBOOKS $0.25 A DAY

$1.00 A DAY

DVDS

I see a lot of different magazines. I love magazines.

"Can I take a magazine home?" I ask the library clerk.

"No, you can't. I'm sorry," she says. "But you can read a magazine here."

I choose an English magazine with many pictures. I try to read a story in the magazine, but it's too hard. The pictures don't help me. I feel frustrated.

A. Mark the sentences T (true) or F (false).

_F_ 1. The library clerk doesn't help Eva.

___ 2. Eva shows her ID card.

___ 3. The man checks out eight books.

___ 4. Eva can't take a magazine home.

___ 5. Eva understands the story in the magazine.

B. Choose *a* or *b*.

1. You have to pay a ___ for late books.

    a. DVD
    b. fine

2. The ___ gives Eva a library card.

    a. library clerk
    b. self-checkout

3. Eva feels ___ because she doesn't understand the story.

    a. happy
    b. frustrated

4. You can listen to a story with ___ .

    a. an audiobook
    b. a magazine

5. This is my first day on the job. I feel ___ .

    a. nervous
    b. sorry

C. Put the pictures in the correct order. Number them from 1 to 3.

_____ a.

_____ b.

_____ c.

What's going to happen next? What do you think? Circle or write your guess.

What is Eva going to do?

a. leave the library

b. check out a magazine

c. look at other things in the library

d. other: _____

Chapter 2

The Job Fair

I look at the name and date on the magazine. I'm going to read the magazine when I know more English.

I want to look at other things in the library. Maybe I can check out an audiobook or a DVD. They can help me learn English.

I walk through the library. I see a man reading a local newspaper. I read the words "Job Fair Today" in the headline. What does *job fair* mean?

I know that a *fair job* has good hours and good pay. But in the headline, the word *fair* comes after the word *job*. What kind of fair does the headline mean? I'm going to ask the library clerk.

"Excuse me, miss, what does *job fair* mean?" I ask the library clerk.

The library clerk smiles. She says, "Many businesses meet in one place. They want to hire people. People go to job fairs to learn about jobs."

I want to know more about the job fair. I need to look at the newspaper again, but the man is still reading.

I'm going to look at the newspaper later.

The pictures in the magazines give me an idea. I want to take home an English picture book. I can read the picture book to my nephew. The pictures can help us learn the words.

"Do you have any picture books?" I ask the library clerk.

"Yes," the library clerk says. "They're in the children's area."

"I want one for my nephew," I say.

A. These sentences are false. Make them true.

1. Eva doesn't want to look at other things in the library.

   <u>Eva wants to look at other things in the library.</u>

2. The man in the library is reading a book.

3. Eva wants a picture book for her niece.

4. The picture books are in the magazine area.

B. Complete the sentences. Use the words in the box.

businesses	job fair	nephew
~~newspaper~~	picture book	

1. I read this ____<u>newspaper</u>____ every day.

2. A _____ is a good gift for a child.

3. Your brother's son is your _____ .

4. This mall has many _____ .

5. A _____ is a good place to look for work.

C. Put the sentences in the correct order. Number them from 1 to 3.

____ a. Eva asks the library clerk what a job fair is.

____ b. Eva reads the words "Job Fair Today."

____ c. Eva wants to look for a picture book.

**What's going to happen next? What do you think?
Read the question. Then circle your guess, *yes* or *no*.**

1. Is Eva going to find a picture book?

   yes   no

2. Is Eva going to a job fair?

   yes   no

3. Is Eva going to work at the library?

   yes   no

4. Is Eva going to ask the library clerk for help?

   yes   no

Chapter 3

Looking for Snow White

I look at the picture books. There are many beautiful books. I love the art. I'm excited. I find some books that I can read to my nephew.

One book is called *Snow White*. I know the story well in Spanish. That's going to help me read the book to my nephew.

I want to find a DVD of *Snow White.* My nephew can watch the story.

I ask the library clerk for help. "How can I find a DVD of *Snow White*?"

"Use the online catalog," the library clerk says. "You can look for the title *Snow White.*"

The library clerk types the letters S-n-o-w W-h-i-t-e into the computer. Then she clicks the Title button. The online catalog lists books called *Snow White*. It lists audiobooks and DVDs, too.

It's fun to find things in the online catalog. I type my last name into the computer. I type V-e-l-a-z-q-u-e-z. I click the Author button. I find books by people with my last name!

Then I click the Subject button. I find two books and an audiobook about an artist. The artist has my last name. I know this artist. When I was ten years old, my grandmother showed me some of his paintings. She said that the artist was in our family. She said that he lived more than 300 years ago.

I'm sure this is the same artist. I want to learn more.

A. Choose the correct answer.

1. Eva finds a picture book called ___ .
   - a. Velazquez
   - b. Snow White
   - c. Spanish

2. The library clerk helps Eva use the ___ .
   - a. job fair
   - b. picture book
   - c. online catalog

3. Eva's grandmother told her about ___ .
   - a. an artist
   - b. an author
   - c. a title

B. Match the pictures with the words.

a.

b.

c.

d.

e.

<u>b</u> 1. author   ___ 4. excited

___ 2. online catalog   ___ 5. artist

___ 3. title

C. What happens first? Circle *a* or *b*.

1. a. Eva finds books about the artist.
   b. Eva types in her last name.

2. a. The library clerk helps Eva.
   b. Eva finds a book called *Snow White*.

3. a. Eva's grandmother tells Eva about the artist.
   b. Eva comes to the library.

What's Next in Chapter 4?

**What's going to happen next? What do you think?
Read the question. Then circle your guess, *yes* or *no*.**

1. Is Eva going to find books about the artist?

   yes   no

2. Is Eva going to visit her grandmother?

   yes   no

3. Is Eva going to meet the artist?

   yes   no

Chapter 4

Many New Worlds

I want to find the books and the audiobook about Velazquez. I look at the computer screen. I write the titles of the two books on a piece of paper. There's a number next to each title. I write the numbers, too.

I take my list to the library clerk. She shows me how to find the books. The numbers tell where the books are.

The first book is too hard. Then I find a book of the artist's paintings. The library clerk helps me find the audiobook.

I love the library. It's a good place to get answers. I'm going to learn more about Velazquez here.

I choose four things to check out. The book and audiobook about Velazquez are for me. The book and DVD about Snow White are for my nephew.

I take everything to the self-checkout. I use my new library card and check out my things.

I pick up my things and walk to the door. I see a sign about the job fair. There are cards under the sign. I take one and look at the address on the card. The job fair is going to be my next stop.

I'm excited. My visit to the library is opening many new worlds for me!

A. Circle the correct answer.

1. What does the number *759.6* tell Eva?
   a. where to find the book
   b. how many pages the book has
   c. when the artist lived

2. How many things does Eva check out?
   a. six
   b. four
   c. one

3. What does Eva see when she leaves the library?
   a. a painting by the artist
   b. a DVD of *Snow White*
   c. a sign for the job fair

B. Choose *a* or *b*.

1. I have a question about this book. I can ask the ____ .
   a. self-checkout
   b. library clerk

2. I'm ready to leave the library. I need to ____ my books.
   a. fill out
   b. check out

3. The ____ on the wall says "No Smoking."
   a. sign
   b. stop

C. Put the pictures in the correct order. Number them from 1 to 4.

a.

_____

b.

_____

c.

_____

d.

_____

What's Next?

Think about what Eva is going to do now.
Write 2 or 3 sentences.

A. Read an application form.

Library Application Form

Name: _Eva Velazquez_

Address: _5616 Alamo Dr._

Austin, TX 78738

Telephone Number: _(512) 555-1234_

Email: _e_velazquez@mail.us_

Signature: _Eva Velazquez_

- Read Eva's library card application form.
- Get a blank application form. It can be from a library, a bank, or another place.
- Read the form. What information do you need?

B. Work with a partner. Fill in the application form.

- Interview your partner. Use the application form to ask questions.
- Write your partner's answers on the form.
- Change roles. Answer your partner's questions.
- Show your application form to the class.

Useful Expressions

"How do you spell your name?"

"What's your address?"

Shared vocabulary from the *OPD*
and *A New World at the Library*

audiobook
[ö**/**dē ō bŏok**/**]

author ⌐
[ö**/**thər]

business
[bĭz**/**nəs]

check out
[chĕk**/**owt**/**]

DVD
[dē**/**vē**/**dē**/**]

excited
[ĭk sī**/**təd]

frustrated
[frŭs**/**trā**/**təd]

headline ⌐
[hĕd**/**līn]

job fair
[jäb**/** fër]

library clerk
[lī/brër ē klürk/]

magazine
[măg/ə zēn/]

nervous
[nür/vəs]

newspaper
[nōōz/pā/pər]

online catalog
[än/līn/ kă/tə lög]

picture book
[pĭk/chər bŏŏk/]

self-checkout
[sĕlf/ chĕk/owt]

title
[tīt/l]

type
[tīp]

A New World at the Library

Eva Velazquez goes to her library. She learns how to use the online catalog. She checks out books. She learns about a job fair!

The nine *Oxford Picture Dictionary* readers are organized into three strands that represent the most common needs and goals of learners. The readers are available separately or as part of a reading library.

		Primary Strand	Secondary Focus
Workplace Reading Library	A Big Night At Maria's Cafe	Workplace	Civics
	Math and Max	Workplace	Academic
	An Important Guest at the Shelton Hotel	Workplace	Civics
Academics Reading Library	A New World at the Library	Academic	Civics
	Annette Succeeds in Class	Academic	Civics
	Healthy Eating	Academic	Workplace
Civics Reading Library	Driving in the City	Civics	Academics
	A Busy Morning at the Bank	Civics	Workplace
	Finding Good Childcare	Civics	Workplace

Also available

- Complete Reading Library (a set of Workplace, Academics, and Civics readers)
- Workplace Reading Library Audio
- Civics Reading Library Audio
- Academics Reading Library Audio
- Complete Reading Library Audio (a set of the Workplace, Academics, and Civics audio)

OXFORD PICTURE DICTIONARY

OPD

OXFORD
UNIVERSITY PRESS

Teacher website provides extra resources, multilevel teaching notes, and reference material
www.oup.com/elt/teacher/opd

ISBN 978-0-19-474030-2

9 780194 740302